D1451496

OCT 0 2 2004

CP

A PRIMARY SOURCE LIBRARY OF AMERICAN CITIZENSHIP™

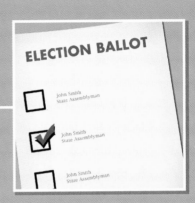

Voting

Tracie Egan

rosen central
Primary Source™

The Rosen Publishing Group, Inc., New York

Published in 2004 by The Rosen Publishing Group, Inc.
29 East 21st Street, New York, NY 10010

Copyright © 2004 by The Rosen Publishing Group, Inc.

First Edition

Library of Congress Cataloging-in-Publication Data

Egan, Tracie.
Voting/by Tracie Egan.—1st ed.
    p. cm.—(A Primary Source Library of American Citizenship)
Includes bibliographical references (p.) and index.
Contents: The history of voting—Registration—Presidential elections—The electoral college.
ISBN 0-8239-4479-4 (library binding)
1. Voting–United States—Juvenile literature. 2. Elections—United States—Juvenile literature.
[1. Voting. 2. Elections.]
I. Title. II. Series.
JK1978.E33 2004
324.6'0973—dc21

                                                                              2003007167
Manufactured in the United States of America

On the cover: At bottom left, residents of Brooklyn, New York, line up to enter voting booths during the presidential election of November 2000. At top right, a group of African Americans on the steps of their local city hall in 1948 urge others to register to vote. In the background is the 1869 congressional resolution ratifying the 15th Amendment to the Constitution, granting African American men the right to vote.

Photo credits: cover (bottom left) © Reuters NewMedia Inc./Corbis; cover (top right), pp. 4, 8, 12, 26 © Library of Congress, Prints and Photographs Division; cover (background) Enrolled Acts and Resolutions of Congress, 1789–1999, General Records of the United States Government, Record Group 11, National Archives; pp. 5, 23 © AFP/Corbis; p. 6 © The Maryland Historical Society, Baltimore, Maryland; p. 7 © William H. English Collection, Special Collections Research Center, University of Chicago Library; p. 9 © Flip Schulke/Corbis; p. 10 © Joseph Sohm; ChromSohm, Inc./Corbis; pp. 11, 13, 14, 15, 16, 17 (top and bottom), 20 © AP/Wide World Photos; p. 19 (top and bottom) © Bettmann/ Corbis; pp. 21, 27 © National Archives and Records Administration, Records of the U.S. Senate; p. 25 © Reuters NewMedia Inc./Corbis; p. 28 © The Art Archive/Jan Vinchom Numismatist Paris/Dagli Orti; p. 29 © The Art Archive/Agora Museum Athens/Dagli Orti.

Designer: Tahara Hasan; Photo Researcher: Peter Tomlinson

Contents

The History of Voting

The United States of America is a democracy. This means that every American is involved in the decisions that the government makes. Voting for political leaders is the best way for an American to have his or her voice heard. Voting is a basic responsibility of every U.S. citizen.

A group of African Americans on the steps of their local city hall urging others to register to vote. The picture was taken in 1948, when the Democratic Party first adopted civil rights provisions in its party platform.

At the age of 101, Neil Tillotson, New Hampshire's oldest resident, casts his vote in the 2001 New Hampshire primary in the town of Dixville Notch.

Any American citizen over 18 years of age may vote in federal elections, as long as he or she meets certain state requirements. But things weren't always this way. At the time of the ratification of the Constitution in 1787, the right to vote was limited mostly to white men who were over 21 years old and owned land.

In the 1790s, slaves work the fields while their overseer looks on. In the early American South, though slaves were not allowed to vote, they were counted in determining representation in Congress.

A voting list for Knox County, Indiana Territory, 1802. An election was held that year to choose delegates for a convention to decide if slavery would be legalized in the territory. The first candidate at the top left was William Henry Harrison, then territorial governor, soon to be the ninth president of the United States.

However, over the next 200 years, amendments were made to the Constitution. These amendments extended the right to vote to more citizens, such as women and nonwhite people. Although all American adults are now able to vote, they cannot do so until they are registered.

The headquarters of the women's suffrage movement in Cleveland, Ohio, 1912. Women did not get the vote until 1920.

After passage of the Voting Rights Act in 1966, these African Americans in Alabama cast their votes for the first time.

ELECTION BALLOT

2 Registration

Registration for voting is different in each state, but it usually involves some forms that need to be filled out. These forms can be found in a state's election office. However, registration forms can also be found at other state offices.

REGISTER HERE
★ ★ ★ ★
VOTER
REGISTRAR

A sign tells citizens where to go to register to vote. Registration helps to determine whether people are eligible to vote and in what electoral districts they should vote.

Texas secretary of state Gwyn Shea explains the electoral process to high school students as part of the state's Project VOTE program.

States have passed laws making registration easier for U.S. citizens. In many states, people are able to register when applying for a driver's license or at an armed forces recruitment office.

President Bill Clinton signs the National Voter Registration Act of 1993, making it easier for voters to register through their motor vehicle registrations.

Juan Argumedo explains a sample ballot to Hispanic voters
before an upcoming primary election in Woodburn, Oregon, in
2002. This was part of a drive to register more Hispanics.

Registration is also offered at places such as public libraries, post offices, unemployment offices, and public high schools and universities. Some states even allow voters to register online through the National Mail Voter Registration Form.

Indiana University students register to vote while on their spring break in Panama City Beach, Florida, in 2002.

Arizona Democratic Party chairman Mark Fleisher clicks his mouse to cast his vote in the first legally binding presidential primary conducted over the Internet in 2000.

3 Presidential Elections

A presidential election is held once every four years. Each political party must nominate candidates for president and vice president. To choose candidates, each party holds primary elections during the election year in each state. This is a voter's first opportunity to help decide who the next president will be.

From left to right, Democratic presidential candidates Jerry Brown, Paul Tsongas, Bob Kerry, Bill Clinton, and Tom Harkin pose in an Arlington, Virginia, television studio before their debate in 1992.

Above, Al Gore campaigns for the presidency in 1999 by talking to sheet metal workers in Manchester, New Hampshire. New Hampshire holds the nation's earliest presidential primary. Below, George W. Bush files papers in Concord, New Hampshire, putting his name on the ballot for the Republican primary.

After winning their party's primary elections, the candidates for each party campaign. They make speeches and hold debates on television to help people decide whom they would like to vote for. The candidates campaign this way up until Election Day. Election Day is the Tuesday after the first Monday in November of the election year.

Election Day

Election Day was set in November because the United States used to be a nation made up mostly of farmers. Harvesting the crops was completed by November, so the farmers were free to travel to vote.

Above, the first televised presidential debates between Richard M. Nixon and John F. Kennedy in October 1960. Below, one of the last old-fashioned "whistle stop" campaign tours by train, conducted by Dwight D. Eisenhower in 1952.

On Election Day, voters can cast their votes. Most people use voting booths that are set up in different areas in their voting district. A voter has the right to keep his or her vote secret. However, the presidency is not decided by popular vote. According to the Constitution, the electoral college decides who the next president will be.

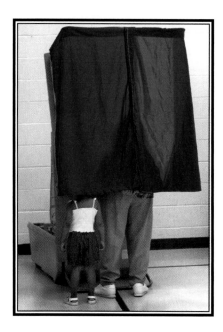

Three-year-old Destinie Vigil stands in a voting booth as her grandmother votes during primary elections in New Mexico, 2002.

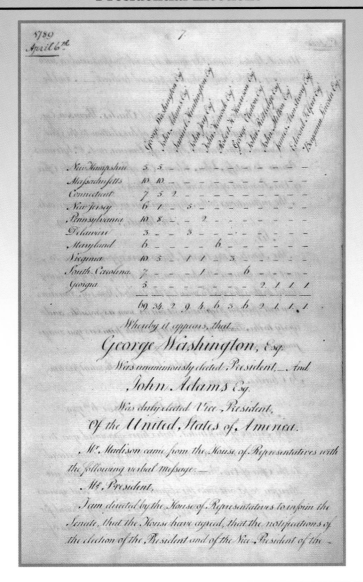

From the *Journal of the Senate*, 1789, these are the results of the vote that elected George Washington and John Adams the first president and vice president of the United States.

4 The Electoral College

Each state is appointed a number of electors for the electoral college. The number of electors is determined by the number of congressional representatives that a state has. When voters step into a voting booth, they are actually voting for electors who have promised to vote for a particular candidate.

The Electors' Choice

Legally, electors in the electoral college are allowed to vote for someone other than the candidate they pledged to vote for. But this usually doesn't happen.

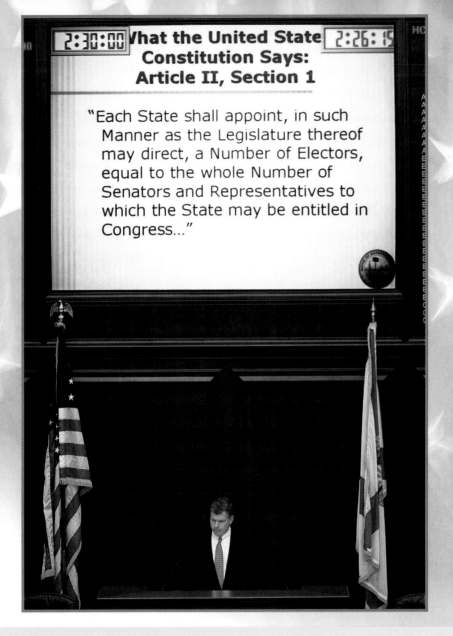

What the United State Constitution Says: Article II, Section 1

"Each State shall appoint, in such Manner as the Legislature thereof may direct, a Number of Electors, equal to the whole Number of Senators and Representatives to which the State may be entitled in Congress..."

Tom Feeney, speaker of the Florida House of Representatives, gives a speech under a screen showing the section of the Constitution authorizing the states to choose electors for the electoral college.

The candidate who receives the most votes in each state will receive all of the state's electoral college votes. In December, the electors meet in their state capital. They cast their ballots and select the new president of the United States. In order to win, a candidate must receive a majority of the votes.

Electoral Votes Count

George W. Bush did not win the popular vote in the 2000 election. He won states with a high number of electors, so he was able to win the presidential election through the electoral college.

Vice President Al Gore *(left)* at a joint session of Congress helps to count the electoral votes for the 2000 presidential election, in which he was beaten by his opponent, George W. Bush.

If no candidate receives a majority, the House of Representatives decides who the next president will be. Although it does not happen often, Congress has had to decide who the president would be in the past. This is how the third president of the United States, Thomas Jefferson, was elected.

Thomas Jefferson, third president of the United States, was elected by the House of Representatives when he failed to win a majority of the electoral college votes.

	Thomas Jefferson of Virginia	Aaron Burr of New York	John Adams of Massachusetts	Charles Cotesworth Pinckney of South Carolina	John Jay of New York
New Hampshire			6	6	
Massachusetts			16	16	
Rhode Island			4	3	1
Connecticut			9	9	
Vermont			4	4	
New York	12	12			
New Jersey			7	7	
Pennsylvania	8	8	7	7	
Delaware			3	3	
Maryland	5	5	5	5	
Virginia	21	21			
Kentucky	4	4			
North Carolina	8	8	4	4	
Tennessee	3	3			
South Carolina	8	8			
Georgia	4	4			
	73	73	65	64	1

A tally of the electoral college votes for the 1800 presidential election between Thomas Jefferson and Aaron Burr. It was a tie. In 1804 the 12th Amendment to the Constitution called for separate elections for president and vice president to avoid this problem.

Voting is one of the most important rights of citizens. Allowing each citizen to vote is what sets the United States apart from many other countries. The United States of America is a true democracy, a government run for the people and by the people.

This silver coin from the time of the Roman Republic depicts a citizen casting his vote by ballot.

This shard of pottery was called an ostracon by the ancient Greeks. It was used as a ballot to vote to ostracize, or exile, leaders thought to be a threat to democracy. This one bears the name of Themistocles, who was exiled from Athens in 480 BC.

Glossary

amendment (uh-MEND-mint) An addition or change to the U. S. Constitution.

ballot (BA-lut) A paper that a vote is recorded on.

campaign (kam-PAYN) When candidates make speeches and travel the country to convince people to vote for them.

candidate (KAN-dih-dayt) A person who is nominated in an election.

citizen (SIH-tih-zen) A person who is a member of a country.

democracy (dih-MAH-kruh-see) A government chosen by the people through elections.

majority (muh-JOR-ih-tee) More than half.

privilege (PRIV-lij) A right or a special benefit.

register (REH-jih-stur) When someone enters into an official list.

representative (reh-prih-ZEN-tah-tiv) A person elected to speak for a group of people.

Web Sites

Due to the changing nature of Internet links, the Rosen Publishing Group, Inc., has developed an online list of Web sites related to the subject of this book. This site is updated regularly. Please use this link to access the list:

http://www.rosenlinks.com/pslac/vote

Primary Source Image List

Page 4: Registering to vote, 1948, from the files of the NAACP, now with the Library of Congress.

Page 5: Neil Tillotson, photographed by Mark E. Johnson for AP, 2000.

Page 6: Watercolor by Benjamin Henry Latrobe, 1798, now with the Baltimore Historical Society.

Page 7: Voting list, Knox County, Indiana Territory, now with the Library of Congress.

Page 8: Women's suffrage headquarters, Cleveland, Ohio, 1902, now with the Library of Congress.

Page 9: Black men voting in Alabama, photographed by Flip Schulke in 1966.

Page 10: Voter registration sign, Buckingham, Virginia, photographed by Joseph Sohm in 1992.

Page 11: Texas secretary of state Gwyn Shea, photographed by D. J. Peters for AP, 2002.

Page 12: Photograph of President Clinton, 1993, now with the Library of Congress.

Page 13: Juan Argumedo, photographed by Greg Wahl-Stephens for AP, 2002.

Page 14: Indiana students register to vote, photographed by Bill Kaczor for AP, 2002.

Page 15: Mark Fleisher, photographed by Roy Dabner for AP, 2000.

Page 16: The 1992 Democratic television debate, photographed by Scott Applewhite for AP, 1992.

Page 17 (top): Al Gore, photographed by Jim Cole for AP, 1999.

Page 17 (bottom): George Bush, photographed by Jim Cole for AP, 1999.

Page 20: Voting booth, New Mexico, photographed by Pat Vasquez-Cunningham for AP, 2002.

Page 21: *Journal of the Senate*, April 6, 1789, now with the Library of Congress.

Page 23: Tom Feeney, photographed by Peter Muhly, 2000.

Page 25: Al Gore, photographed by Larry Downing for Reuters, 2000.

Page 26: Portrait of Thomas Jefferson, lithograph published by H. Robinson, New York and Washington, now with the Library of Congress.

Page 27: Vote tally for the 1800 presidential election, now with the National Archives and Records Administration.

Page 28: Roman coin, minted prior to 44 BC, from Jan Vinchon Numismatist, Paris.

Page 29: Terra-cotta pottery shard, from fifth century BC Greece, now with the Agora Museum in Athens.

Index

About the Author

Tracie Egan is a freelance writer who lives in Brooklyn, New York.